insomnia

insomnia

DANIEL BROOKS
WITH
GUILLERMO VERDECCHIA

Insomnia
first published 1999 by
Scirocco Drama
An imprint of J. Gordon Shillingford Publishing Inc.
© 1999 Daniel Brooks with Guillermo Verdecchia

Scirocco Drama Series Editor: Dave Carley
Cover illustration by Lisa Kiss
Cover design by Terry Gallagher/Doowah Design Inc.
Author photo by Guntar Kravis
Printed and bound in Canada

We acknowledge the support of The Canada Council for the Arts and the Manitoba Arts Council for our publishing program.

All rights reserved. No part of this book may be reproduced, for any reason, by any means, without the permission of the publisher. This play is fully protected under the copyright laws of Canada and all other countries of the Copyright Union and is subject to royalty. Changes to the text are expressly forbidden without written consent of the authors. Rights to produce, film, record in whole or in part, in any medium or in any language, by any group amateur or professional, are retained by the authors.
Production inquiries should be addresses to:
da da kamera, 401 Richmond Street West, Suite 363
Toronto, ON M5V 3A8

Canadian Cataloguing in Publication Data

Brooks, Daniel, 1958–
    Insomnia

A play.
ISBN 1-896239-54-4

    I. Verdecchia, Guillermo II. Title.

PS8553.R658157 1999   C812'.54   C99-901190-1
PR9199.3.B69717157 1999

For Jennifer

Guillermo Verdecchia and Daniel Brooks

About the Authors

Daniel Brooks is an accomplished director, writer, actor, and teacher, considered to be at the forefront of Canada's new generation of theatre artists. Co-artistic director of da da kamera and founder of the Augusta Company, he is a recipient of the Pauline McGibbon award for outstanding direction, the Edinburgh Fringe First award, two Chalmers awards for new Canadian plays and three Dora Mavor Moore awards.

Guillermo Verdecchia is a writer, director, and actor whose work has been seen and heard across Canada and around the world. The author or co-author of, among other works, *Fronteras Americanas*, *The Noam Chomsky Lectures* (with Daniel Brooks) and *A Line in the Sand* (with Marcus Youssef), he is a recipient of the Governor General's Literary Award for Drama, a four-time winner of the Chalmers Canadian Play Award, as well as a recipient of Dora, Jessie, and sundry film festival awards.

Production History

Insomnia was first produced by the Augusta Company in association with the Theatre Centre in Toronto, May 20-June 1, 1997. It was presented as "a work in progress" with the following cast:

JOHN F.	Daniel Brooks
GWEN	Tamsin Kelsey
WILLIAM	Guillermo Verdecchia
KATE	Fiona Highet

Directed by Guillermo Verdecchia with Daniel Brooks
Consulting Director: Daniel MacIvor
Designed by Julie Fox
Sound and Music by Richard Feren
Lighting Consultant: Andrea Lundy
Stage Manager: Melissa Berney
Assistant: Chad Donella
Producers: Daniel Brooks and David Duclos

Insomnia was revised and subsequently produced by the Augusta Company and the Theatre Centre at the Theatre Centre, October 7-25, 1998 with the following cast:

JOHN F.	Daniel Brooks
GWEN	Fiona Highet
WILLIAM	Randy Hughson
KATE	Lisa Ryder

Directed by Guillermo Verdecchia with Daniel Brooks
Set and Costume Design by Julie Fox
Sound and Music by Richard Feren
Lighting by Andrea Lundy
Stage Manager: Melissa Berney
Assistant Director: Chad Donella
Producers: Daniel Brooks and David Duclos

Acknowledgements

We would like to thank Daniel MacIvor and John Mighton for their generous input, particularly regarding the structure of the play.

Also, thanks to Tracy Wright, Sarah Stanley and Jonathan Wilson who participated in an early workshop of the script.

Special thanks to David Duclos, who encouraged and supported *Insomnia* before there were words on paper, and continued to do so throughout the process of creation.

Final thanks to the Tarragon Theatre, where much of *Insomnia* was written, and Sherrie Johnson for her relentless support.

Characters

JOHN F.
GWEN (his common law wife)
WILLIAM (his brother)
KATE (William's wife)

Setting

The set for the original production was a deep forced perspective, 54 feet deep, with heavy black curtains on either side. Four corridors cut laterally across the playing area. The floor was painted red. On the upstage wall, approximately 10 feet above the stage floor, was a small window. Through the window a crib, a mobile, and a lamp were visible. The lamp was sometimes on, sometimes off. The only furniture on the stage was a large shabby black armchair.

Notes on the Text

The following is as much a document of a performance as it is a written play. The text, choreography, and design are parts of a whole. The play is still being performed as of publication. As a result, the following text is subject to change, and it is recommended that anyone interested in performing *Insomnia* contact the writers to learn of any amendments to the text.

insomnia

(*The sound of ticking.*

Lights up. JOHN F. is crossing the stage, muttering to himself. He exits. Re-enters with small tape recorder.)

JOHN F: Doubt. Doubt.

(*Presses record. Speaks into recorder.*)

How can you know? How can you be sure? A person never knows.

You don't know, for example, the poisons you ingest day to day. You don't know what cancer you're breathing in this dirty room, ticking minutes off your life with each second accelerating death.

GWEN: (*On mic, offstage.*) It's a baby.

JOHN F: (*Pacing, moving upstage.*) The acceleration of books and knowledge and memories and mistakes—

GWEN: (*On mic, offstage.*) It's a baby.

JOHN F: and more and more and time and death—

GWEN: (*On mic, offstage.*) Decide.

JOHN F: —and how can you know, and who's to blame and the world is dying and what am I doing?

(*JOHN F. turns as GWEN enters.*)

GWEN: It's a baby.

(*Music.*)

It's a baby. It will be a beautiful baby. I'll tell you what. It's time. We may feel we're not ready but when will we ever be ready? Take this match book and write your answer on the inside. Whatever you decide.

(He takes the matchbook. Writes on it. Gives it to GWEN. She looks, smiles. He smiles, places his hand on her belly. They move to kiss. Before their lips touch an alarm sounds sharply. JOHN F. snaps his head away and begins to slowly walk towards audience, half asleep, muttering. GWEN exits. A TV crosses. WILLIAM and KATE enter from opposite sides, meet centre stage, kiss, walk upstage. They pass by JOHN F. A standing lamp crosses, turns on, is placed by the big chair. GWEN re-enters, sits in the big chair. JOHN F. continues toward audience, spits out a tooth, stops, looks up.

Blackout. Ticking.)

(Lights up. JOHN F. reads a newspaper on the floor.

GWEN reads a magazine in the big chair. Chews potato chips loudly. JOHN F. annoyed. She licks her fingers noisily. JOHN F. returns to the newspaper. She crunches chips. He looks at her. She stops, extends the bag to him.)

GWEN: Want some?

(JOHN F. places the newspaper aside, takes the chips, places them aside, takes the magazine, places it aside, moves to GWEN.)

JOHN F: Want some, uh, what?

GWEN: What?

JOHN F: *(He fondly fondles her.)* How 'bout a little uh—

GWEN: I'm too tired.

JOHN F: *(Disappointed.)* Oh.

GWEN: I'm getting a cold. I'm just getting over pneumonia.

JOHN F: That wasn't pneumonia.

GWEN: Whatever. *(Cough.)* And Lilly's coming down with something. You know, people never used to get sick.

JOHN F: Sure they did.

GWEN: No, you—there are people who'd go 17 years without ever getting sick. You never hear that now.

JOHN F: That's because when they got sick they died.

GWEN: I'd rather die at 57 than go through this twice a year.

JOHN F: *(Trying to unbutton her pants.)* They'd die at 32.

GWEN: I don't think people got as sick.

JOHN F: And how do you know. Where do you hear this from?

GWEN: Anecdotal—

JOHN F: *(Overlaps.)* anecdotal, right

GWEN: *(Overlaps above.)* —evidence I guess.

JOHN F: Well I'd like to see the hard research.

GWEN: Well—

JOHN F: There's also the matter of the bubonic plague, the pox that wiped out whole civilizations, infant mortality rates. I mean, its easy to rail against western medicine but—

(GWEN coughs.)

...sorry.

GWEN: I'd rather be dead.

JOHN F: C'mon, let's have some fun. *(Begins to paw her.)*

GWEN: No, really, I'm coming down with something.

JOHN F: I was hoping you'd be going down on something.

GWEN: You are such a jerk.

JOHN F: I'll settle for a jerk.

GWEN: Are William and Kate coming tomorrow?

JOHN F: As far as I know.

GWEN: How far is that?

JOHN F: All the way.

GWEN: I'm not cooking for them.

JOHN F: We'll go out.

GWEN: We can't afford it.

JOHN F: He'll pay.

GWEN: He always pays. It's embarrassing. And who's gonna take care of Lilly?

JOHN F: Honey, William is rich, it's nothing to him.

GWEN: I don't know.

JOHN F: Sushi, miso, sake…

GWEN: All right.

JOHN F: Excellent. *(He stops pawing her and stands.)* Let's celebrate. Between the sheets in five. *(He begins to leave.)*

GWEN: I'm really beat.

(He doesn't leave.

Beat. Blackout. Shift.)

(Lights. Upstage a television, turned on, showing static. JOHN F. on the floor. GWEN in the big chair. They look forward, at the same spot, as if watching television.)

GWEN: …You know I have desires too.

JOHN F: I'm sure. Why don't you go ahead and do whatever it is you desire to do?

GWEN: It's not that easy.

JOHN F: What is it? Do you want to have an affair? *(JOHN F. takes small tape recorder and sets it up as he speaks.)*

Do you wanna run away to Japan, have orgies with relatives— *(He presses record.)*

—what?

GWEN: What are you doing?

JOHN F: Uh, it's just um…for the record. That's OK, isn't it? …It's not?

GWEN: Wha—what are you doing?

JOHN F: Well, I ah, want to have a record.

GWEN: A record?

JOHN F: Yeah. To remember what we say.

GWEN: Why?

JOHN F: Well—

GWEN: To remember what we say?

JOHN F: Well, you ah—I mean…it's hard to explain. I—

GWEN: You want to record our conversation?

JOHN F: No, not exactly.

GWEN: Not exactly?

JOHN F:	No. I had a notion... OK. A man has an argument with his wife. He leaves in a rage, gets in his car, drives away, turns on the radio, and hears the fight he just had with his wife—word for word—on public radio. He listens, and then he begins to laugh.
GWEN:	...Ha ha.
JOHN F:	You're not going to play with me here? He begins to laugh because—
GWEN:	I'm not interested. What do you intend to do with it?
JOHN F:	I want to listen to it, so I can hear what we say to each other.
GWEN:	Not quick enough to get it the first time round?
JOHN F:	No I'm not.
GWEN:	Are you writing something?
JOHN F:	I don't know.
GWEN:	Are you writing something?
JOHN F:	I will not be censored by you, I'm—
GWEN:	You are. I do not wan— I will not be used for dialogue. Right? Understand?

(JOHN F. turns off the tape. Sets the recorder aside. Faces television.)

JOHN F:	I'll stop. I won't do it anymore.
GWEN:	Anymore?
JOHN F:	I mean I'll stop I mean. I'll stop recording.
GWEN:	And I'll start.
JOHN F:	Start what?

GWEN: I don't know, we'll see.

JOHN F: Ooo, that's ominous… So. You were saying? Sorry. Go on. You were talking about…what were we talking about?

GWEN: Didn't catch it on tape?

JOHN F: No.

GWEN: I was talking about my desire—

JOHN F: Your desires. Sorry. Go on.

(Beat. Blackout. Shift.)

(Lights up. GWEN standing. JOHN F. in the big chair, reclining.)

JOHN F: But how do you know?

GWEN: I read it.

JOHN F: Oh well then.

GWEN: Why do you talk like that?

JOHN F: Like what?

GWEN: There is no flow to the conversation.

JOHN F: I'm skeptical. I can't help it.

GWEN: There's no discussion with you.

JOHN F: But how do you know?

GWEN: What?

JOHN F: That some C.E.O. from the tobacco industry admitted that the industry has knowingly lied?

GWEN: I told you I read it.

JOHN F: Where?

GWEN: I don't remember.

JOHN F: It's just something you may have read somewhere, but you don't know. And besides, the book or magazine was sold to you—

GWEN: Here we go—

JOHN F: Sold to you to sell advertising or make a buck for the writer who may or may not be compromised. And even the best of us has an opinion to sell, some stake in being right, so—

GWEN: So how many Jews were killed in the war?

JOHN F: Well...exactly.

GWEN: Have you ever had any proof, absolute proof?

JOHN F: Exactly.

GWEN: Hearsay, doctored photos, exaggerated stories by people who have something to sell.

JOHN F: OK.

GWEN: You're the one who talks about the lie of Israel.

JOHN F: OK.

GWEN: But it's true.

JOHN F: I know, but you sound like you believe it.

GWEN: Well, if I follow what you say, the lack of certainty—

JOHN F: What, you believe that?

GWEN: We can't be sure of anything, so how do—

JOHN F: What, are you a holocaust denier?

   (Pause.)

GWEN: Take a chill pill. *(They regard one another.)* A person never knows.

(Beat. Blackout. Shift.)

(Lights up. GWEN in the chair; JOHN F. on his way offstage.)

JOHN F: Can I get you anything?

GWEN: Forget it.

JOHN F: *(Stops.)* What's wrong?

GWEN: You're being nice to me.

JOHN F: Oh. Well, I ah made a decision.

GWEN: What?

JOHN F: I've decided to be nice.

GWEN: Why?

JOHN F: It's nice to be nice.

GWEN: You better start doing it on a consistent basis. For your daughter. Better teach her how a man is supposed to treat a woman, or else she'll end up stuck with a guy like you.

JOHN F: A guy like me?

GWEN: Yeah.

JOHN F: Mr. Nice Guy?

GWEN: How long is that going to last? William and Kate are coming tomorrow.

JOHN F: And?

GWEN: And you always treat me like shit when your brother's in town, like I'm not good enough for you, like it's my fault.

JOHN F: Fault?

GWEN: You know.

JOHN F: No I don't.

GWEN: Oh don't get all semiotic on me. I don't even know why we're together. We are totally incompatible.

JOHN F: Do you want to separate? ...Do you want to separate?

GWEN: I want you to be nice to me.

JOHN F: I've already told you I've decided to be nice.

GWEN: And I've already told you it's not gonna last.

JOHN F: Listen, you have to decide if you want to stay together. It's you. Decide what you want to do, take as long as you want. We can stay together or—

GWEN: And what would that get us?

JOHN F: I don't know. Twenty years of haggling and ill health and I'll die an early and by you celebrated death of heart cancer, or twenty years to explore each other and work through our infantile problems and cultivate a deep and everlasting love in which the days pass in quiet harmonious contemplation well into a rewarding old age.

Or we can separate, and I'll go through a series of women and repeat the same mistakes and eventually surrender to the reality of my condition and hang myself.

Or I'll meet someone who makes me gloriously happy and proves to me I'm not wrong and Lilly adjusts, or she doesn't, and you treat me like shit every time we meet and make every interaction miserable and you go through a bunch of men and one of them molests Lilly and I end up in the slammer for manslaughter. Or you find that in fact you like living alone and we develop a strong friendship and raise Lilly with mature and intelligent cooperation. Who knows what will happen? I don't. But you've got to think about it and decide because I can't live like this anymore.

GWEN: (*Pause.*) I'm not cooking for them.

JOHN F: Fine, we'll go out.

GWEN: We can't afford it.

JOHN F: He'll pay.

GWEN: He always pays. It's embarrassing. And who's gonna take care of Lilly?

JOHN F: William is my brother. He's had a very good year. It's nothing to him...

(*He waits for a response. She remains silent. He moves to leave.*)

GWEN: Where are you going?

JOHN F: (*He stops.*) I'm gonna go, uh, work.

GWEN: Well just don't have a bath at five in the morning.

JOHN F: Fine.

GWEN: And don't slap your body for five minutes.

JOHN F: Fine. I'll be quiet ... Good night.

GWEN: Now I feel guilty.

JOHN F: It's fine. Don't worry. Think about it. And if you need to ask me anything— (*Joking.*) If you want to know who's to blame, I'll tell you. Anytime.

GWEN: (*Not joking.*) Who's to blame?

(*Beat. Blackout. Shift.*)

(*Lights up. They stand on opposite sides of the big chair.*)

GWEN: You always say that.

JOHN F: Always. Its always "always never" *(Overlaps.)* "always never"

GWEN: *(Overlaps above.)* Yeah yeah always never well I'm sick sick sick of this conventional—it's so fucking boring.

JOHN F: Then leave me.

GWEN: I hate how boring it is. It's so fucking boring.

JOHN F: Then leave.

GWEN: It's like I believed you. I was some funky fucked up anarchist chick and you tamed me—

JOHN F: *(Under her.)* I tamed you.

GWEN: —but I see it now, you are so conventional—

JOHN F: *(Under.)* I'm conventional.

GWEN: I hate the music you play it's fucking boring—

JOHN F: *(Under.)* If I'm so conventional then bite me, bite me.

GWEN: — and your friends are and your father bores me. He doesn't even respect me, he doesn't. What gives him the right? He doesn't know shit about me. And your mother was boring when she was alive, with her paintings all over the place and you are sick, why do you only have time for people who don't need your help and never for people who do? Your father doesn't need help, he's fine, he's happy that your mother finally died. He had hundreds of friends helping him out, but I need it and you can't give it to me. Kate said the same thing about you.

JOHN F: What?

GWEN: That you—well she doesn't get it. Why are you so afraid of your father?

JOHN F: She said that? What—what else does she say about me?

GWEN: It doesn't matter. You're nuts. You know I'm having trouble sleeping and yet you slosh around in the bath at five a.m. I mean is that sane behaviour? I asked Bea and Lauri and they said they'd go nuts.

JOHN F: You asked— *(Stops.)*

GWEN: I had to talk to someone to convince myself I wasn't going insane.

JOHN F: Why—is—does everybody talk about me?

GWEN: People talk to keep themselves sane. We compare notes.

JOHN F: You compare notes with these women you have contempt for—

GWEN: *(Following dialogue overlaps.)* —and now you're studying fucking law—

JOHN F: —these conventional women—

GWEN: —what's that?—

JOHN F: —these friends you hate—

GWEN: —you gonna become a lawyer—

JOHN F: —talk to these conventional women—

GWEN: —you won't talk to me.

JOHN F: —you don't want to talk to me— *(End overlap.)*

GWEN: —you don't talk to me—

JOHN F: —I'M TALKING TO YOU NOW... I'm talking to you now... God, I hate this dirty room.

(Beat. Blackout. Shift.)

(Lights up. JOHN F. is sitting on the arm of the big chair. He unscrews the lightbulb from the standing lamp. GWEN approaches the chair and sits on the other arm, her back to JOHN F.)

JOHN F: Last night I dreamt I went to the cemetery to talk to my mother.

GWEN: What did she say?

JOHN F: I did all the talking.

GWEN: Anyway it doesn't work. It's too late.

JOHN F: Sorry?

(He screws the bulb back into lamp. It works.)

GWEN: Too late. I'm leaving you. Or should I say you're leaving me.

JOHN F: I'm leaving you?

GWEN: That's right. You're leaving me. Where are you going?

JOHN F: I don't know, you're the one with the—

GWEN: Oh fuck off.

JOHN F: I don't know, where should I go?

GWEN: Because I have had it. I'm looking elsewhere.

JOHN F: Do you mean it this time, or…because I thought we were doing quite well.

GWEN: Think what you want, I'm leaving—you're leaving.

JOHN F: Is that what you want? …Well?

GWEN: When was the last time you told me you loved me?

JOHN F: I—

GWEN:	I'll tell you when. December last year. You were drunk and had just told me how sexy you thought Kate was.
JOHN F:	That may…
GWEN:	Do you remember that? You probably don't, do you? Do you?
JOHN F:	Well …
GWEN:	You're—you're… What were you doing up at five this morning, with your activities.
JOHN F:	Act—
GWEN:	There was an aquarium.
JOHN F:	It was just a bath.
GWEN:	It was just a bath.
JOHN F:	That's all I just took a bath *(Overlaps.)* if you don't want me to take a bath I won't do it in the morning—
GWEN:	*(Overlaps above.)* Just a bath just a bath just a bath I don't care— *(End overlap.)* no, you won't take a bath. What is it, why can't you sleep? I—this was the busiest day of my life and you've ruined it and I haven't had a decent sleep in weeks. I can't take it anymore, I can't take it anymore…
	(JOHN F. puts his hand on her shoulder.)
	(She rejects.) What?
	(He withdraws.)
	What? Don't try to reason with me. I'm exhausted. And William is coming tomorrow.
JOHN F:	Do you want me to tell him not to come?
GWEN:	Why don't you leave me, why don't you have the courage to leave me?

JOHN F: It's our child. It's Lilly. I like living with her. I love her. I can't imagine not waking up in the same house as her. I can't imagine not living with her day to day, and I can't imagine working out the details of a separation with you.

(GWEN weeps. Pause. Ticking.)

I'm sorry... I don't know... I just...

(She stands, turns upstage, and slowly exits.

WILLIAM enters in the shadows. GWEN is gone.)

(Lights shift. A big sound. Lights up on WILLIAM. JOHN F. runs to meet him.)

JOHN F: *(Calling upstage.)* William.

WILLIAM: Hey little brother!

(JOHN F. goes to hug him but WILLIAM interrupts.)

Do you believe in love?

JOHN F: What?

WILLIAM: Do you believe in love?

JOHN F: William, you're just off the plane and—

WILLIAM: I believe you can create love out of nothing, just like that. By saying it. "I love you." See? Magic. You say it.

JOHN F: I love you. But that's easy, it rolls off my tongue—

WILLIAM: Rolled off my tongue on the plane. I met a—never mind. Do you love Gwen?

JOHN F: Sure.

WILLIAM: Because you think you should?

JOHN F: What do you mean?

WILLIAM: Because you think you should love your wife? Or because you have a fundamental urge to join with her, something in your stomach that hungers for her and only her.

JOHN F: William, give me a break.

WILLIAM: Do you think a man should love his wife?

JOHN F: I think that love is probably good for a marriage, yeah.

WILLIAM: Where did you get that idea?

JOHN F: It beats hate.

WILLIAM: Not necessarily. I love my wife.

You see, the world is a master hypnotist. Some jerk writes a Bible, someone else sings a song, someone makes a movie and before you know it, multitudes are hypnotized into thinking they have to love their wives or else see a therapist. But it's all hypnosis. You've been hypnotized into believing in love, truth, equality, freedom and a bunch of other cheesy notions invented by Hebrews, Greeks and Frenchmen.

But is there a woman on this earth you do love?

(Sound of chimes.)

I know you'd never commit adultery, because abstaining is honourable, and women love that, and you want to be loved, but is there a woman you hunger for? Your secret is safe.

JOHN F: No, I—

WILLIAM: Now try this: I hate you. Look at me and say, "I hate you".

JOHN F: William, what are you—

WILLIAM: *(Overlaps.)* I'm trying to make a point—

JOHN F: *(Overlaps above.)* We haven't even—

WILLIAM: C'mon, do it. *(End overlap.)*

JOHN F: All right, all right. I hate you.

WILLIAM: No. Look me in the eye, and say it.

JOHN F: William—

WILLIAM: John, say it. For me.

JOHN F: *(Weakly.)* …I hate you.

WILLIAM: Oh, please…

JOHN F: *(For real.)* …I hate you.

WILLIAM: Ahh it's a wonderful life. *(WILLIAM moves.)* The place looks great.

JOHN F: No it doesn't.

WILLIAM: Why did you ask me to come?

JOHN F: I didn't ask you to come.

WILLIAM: Why did you "summon" me then? *(Pause.)* Where's Gwen?

JOHN F: Out with Lilly.

WILLIAM: *(Mocking.)* Out with Lilly. How did you come up with a name like Lilly anyway? I can't think of anyone interesting with that name.

JOHN F: It uh, we just, um—we liked it.

WILLIAM: Uh huh.

JOHN F: Where's Kate?

WILLIAM: She has some business with Gordon's estate.

JOHN F: She's not coming?

WILLIAM:	She'll be here tomorrow. *(Exits.)*
JOHN F:	Good. You hungry?
WILLIAM:	*(Enters, eating a banana.)* No. How's Gwen?
JOHN F:	Fine. How are things at Disney?
WILLIAM:	Great. You've never approved, have you?
JOHN F:	No, sure, you ah, we all do what we have to do, and I'm sure *(Overlap.)* there's plenty of—
WILLIAM:	*(Overlaps above.)* Hey hey hey hey— You don't have to do that for me. You know, Kate has always said…
JOHN F:	What?
WILLIAM:	Nothing… How's your thing going?
JOHN F:	My…?
WILLIAM:	That ah—what are you working on?
JOHN F:	Oh, my uh, whatever, my opus.
WILLIAM:	My opus. Trouble with your eyes?
JOHN F:	My opus. Ha.
WILLIAM:	*(Quiet.)* You fuck.
JOHN F:	What?
WILLIAM:	What?
JOHN F:	You said something, I just didn't—
WILLIAM:	I did? I don't know what. I say things, I find I just say things since I quit smoking, things just fall out of my mouth and I think it's because I don't have a cigarette as a cork. And half the time I don't know what I'm saying or doing, I just say it and do it. How's Gwen?

JOHN F: Fine. William, what are you—?

WILLIAM: You think I don't know.

JOHN F: Know what?

WILLIAM: You think you've kept your secret.

JOHN F: What secret?

WILLIAM: That secret. The terrible secret of a troubled marriage. Do you want to talk?

JOHN F: No, there's no point, we just aren't having much, um, the fun is ah—it's funless. Anyway I don't want to talk.

WILLIAM: How's the sex?

JOHN F: The sex is fine. Sex is…fine.

WILLIAM: Why don't you leave her?

JOHN F: I can't.

WILLIAM: Why not?

JOHN F: I can't afford it. It's easy for people with money, but—

WILLIAM: Do you need money? I can give you money.

JOHN F: We also have a child.

WILLIAM: If you didn't would you leave her?

JOHN F: We have a child—

WILLIAM: But if you didn't *(Overlap.)* would you leave—

JOHN F: *(Overlaps above.)* —we have a child—

WILLIAM: Yeah—

JOHN F: —and divorce damages kids. The statistics are there. And besides, we're trying…to work it out,

	we are. There's just so much pressure. If we could only get some money *(Overlap.)* or some—
WILLIAM:	*(Overlaps above.)* —I've told—I've told you I can give you money.
JOHN F:	I don't want your money, I want my own. Something has to change... Can you get me a job at Disney?
WILLIAM:	What?
JOHN F:	Can you get me a job at Disney? I'm serious. I'd like to make some changes.
WILLIAM:	Changes? You'd have to change everything. I'll have to teach you how to walk again. You'd have to unlearn everything you know, relearn how you smile, what you think when you look at the moon, how you kiss your child in the morning, re-circuit your brain. I—I - I, ah, I don't think so. You're better off ... OK, what's the opus on?
JOHN F:	On?
WILLIAM:	On, about, c'mon, don't fuck with me.
JOHN F:	Democracy.
WILLIAM:	Christ, I don't think you have the will to make a dime.
JOHN F:	I'm throbbing pulsating will, something's gotta change I need to make some money.
WILLIAM :	No, I don't think so. I think you want to save the world, don't you? Me, I have no problem, I'm comfortable in my corruption. But you, you want to save the world. Forget money. Go with what you know. Let's get going on the save the world project. Wanna make a difference? C'mon, let's do it, let's go, tick tock, money you want I can help. Just ask. I'm here, you've asked me to come I am here, what is it that you want me to do?

There are no limits, only in what you have courage to do so take for God's sakes. You know how much money I made this year? ...No? Neither do I. My accountant does. But I know how much he makes. Always know how much your accountant makes. How much did you make?

JOHN F: Not much, that's why I'm—

WILLIAM : Who cares, it's not about money. Get that through your head. Making money is math, nothing more. How do you feel about showing your body to your daughter?

JOHN F: Well…what do you mean?

WILLIAM: Do you let her see your penis or do you hide?

JOHN F: I guess I hide.

WILLIAM: I let Gracia see mine. One day I said, "Gracia, this is my penis." She lost interest. Did I do the right thing? You tell me.

JOHN F: Seems fine. I'm just too modest.

WILLIAM: You see I think a child should know. The more you know the less you fear. You conquer one mystery you can move on to another, and the universe is filled with an infinitude of mysteries.

Maybe I'm wrong. Did I do my daughter damage?

JOHN F: I have no idea.

WILLIAM: *(Grabs JOHN F.'s chin.)* Have you ever damaged me? Damage… Damage, John, it's the way of the world. Your child will be damaged no matter what you do. You're damaged. Do some damage. It's time for you to damage. Vengeance. Grab some power, break some windows. Be a terrorist, hurt someone. The world John, the gaping maw of pleasure that is out there, the glorious world John, it's calling, can't you hear it? "John" it calls—

(JOHN F. laughs, WILLIAM grabs him by shoulders.)

take me John, eat me, fuck me, do me, because you're going to die, really soon, really soon, and things are exactly the way they are supposed to be so stop whining you stupid whining sniveling fuck.

(Slamming him into chair.) Stop whining, stop talking and stop whining and wake up. WAKE UP!

(WILLIAM slams JOHN F. violently into chair and releases him.)

Big sound. WILLIAM exits. Big shift.)

JOHN F: *(Muttering.)* Gordon...Kate's love...then not...doubt...suicide...William...Gordon and Kate...Kate and William and Gordon...the combinations, the numbers, conspiracies, RRSPs...

(His voice begins to repeat on speakers.) ...mine are 6 to 9 percent...the house...seven point six percent on one hundred thousand and that's taxed, in RRSP it's 3 to 9 at whatever and the tax isn't there

(His voice continues repeating on speakers, beginning to loop and echo.) but the rates have dropped two percent on seven point six...two...so I've already lost...that's irrelevant I haven't lost anything...

(Voice increasingly looped and echoing.) Tai chi is 27. I'll have to drop that and utilities at 150 I can't even afford a hot bath Gwen's gonna have to pick up, let's see, 300 unless we add 500 for downstairs and the dentist 3 times 127, oh fuck the dentist, fuck the dentist ...

(KATE drifts in far upstage. She holds a suitcase. Sings. Her singing overlaps with the end of looping and echoing.)

KATE: (*Singing.*) Who's gonna shoe your pretty little feet?
Who's gonna glove your little hand.
And who's gonna kiss, your ruby red lips?
Oooo, ooo, ooo, ooo.

JOHN: Kate?

KATE: Poppa's gonna shoe your pretty little feet.
Momma's gonna glove your little hands.
And I'm gonna kiss your ruby red lips.
Ooo, ooo, ooo, ooo.

> (*The sound of an airplane takes over. JOHN F. snaps out of reverie and exits. Enters further upstage reading newspaper. Crosses quickly. Exits. Sound of airplane louder. JOHN F. enters further upstage, chewing donut, in a hurry. Crosses and exits. Sound of airplane louder. KATE slowly moves downstage, looking for someone. JOHN F. enters upstage of KATE, running across, exits. Sound of a bell, airplane stops, JOHN F. immediately enters. Waves to KATE.*)

JOHN F: (*Calls.*) Kate. (*Walks to her.*) Hi. You look great.

KATE: Where's William?

JOHN F: Waiting in the car.

KATE: Did you guys get a car?

JOHN F: No. William rented one.

> (*She walks, JOHN F. follows.*)

You look…great. Thin.

KATE: Haven't lost any weight.

JOHN F: Well, you look svelte. Svelte is the word I'd use.

KATE: Thanks, I guess. You look…fatigued.

> (*She exits. He follows. She enters, waits. He follows.*)

JOHN F: How's Gracia?

(They step onto moving sidewalk.)

KATE: Perfect. We have a new nanny and she is wonderful. She has a PhD in child education. Gracia adores her. Zlata.

JOHN F: Zlata. Yugoslavian?

KATE: Serbian. She had to get out. And we found her. How's Gwen? Lilly?

JOHN F: Good *(Pause.)* Let me take your bag.

KATE: That's all right. You take your present. *(Gives him a bottle.)* There's magic inside.

JOHN F: Thanks. How was the flight?

(They step off moving sidewalk.)

KATE: I don't know. I slept the whole way.

JOHN F: Any dreams?

KATE: Nothing …

(She exits. He follows.

A series of crosses: WILLIAM appears. Greets KATE when she re-enters, takes her suitcase. They kiss. JOHN F. re-enters, reading newspaper, goes the wrong way.)

WILLIAM: This way John.

(JOHN F. follows. WILLIAM exits. Throws suitcase at JOHN from offstage. JOHN F. catches and follows. Car crosses the stage. JOHN F. follows, out of breath, lugging suitcase. He exits.

Light shift.)

(Hotel. A small chair in the middle of the stage. KATE sits. WILLIAM paces.)

KATE: I'll take the car at seven.

WILLIAM: And I'll meet you at eleven.

KATE: Good.

WILLIAM: ...There's something I'd like you to do for me.

KATE: What?

WILLIAM: I have an idea. I want to do something to John. And Gwen too, I think, to...

KATE: What do you have in mind?

WILLIAM: I'm not sure yet.

KATE: Not sure. You remind me of John when you talk like that.

WILLIAM: Is that so?

KATE: Mmmmm. Let me look at you...

(She takes his arm. He moves away.)

What is it? Why are you so restless?

WILLIAM: I'm hungry.

KATE: Order room service.

WILLIAM: No.

KATE: No?

WILLIAM: No. I'm hungry for something, I don't know... different.

KATE: What?

WILLIAM: A poison blowfish or a sea turtle. Some endangered species. Something worth eating. Something you hunt with your own hands and eat raw, I don't know. I was thinking how there are so few real experiences now. Everything is prepared, organised, understood. I have a longing for some real experience. I'm hungry for reality. I could eat you ...

(KATE stares off.)

Kate.

KATE: Hmm?

WILLIAM: What can I do? What can I possibly do to keep you interested?

KATE: Sorry, I was just thinking.

WILLIAM: About?

KATE: Nothing...

WILLIAM: I'm hungry. *(He exits.)*

(Sound. Shift.)

(KATE slowly walks downstage. The sound of chimes. JOHN F. slowly crosses to where she was, as if she were still there. He crosses and exits. She sits in the big chair. GWEN enters.

Sound. Shift.)

GWEN: Where's Lilly?

KATE: Shhh. She's sleeping.

GWEN: You got her down?

KATE: She's easy. Did you clear your head?

GWEN: I smoked seven cigarettes in one hour. I feel great. I can't remember the last time I had a break.

KATE: Doesn't John—

GWEN: John? John's too busy. John's too tired. You know all he has to do is say he's tired and—I don't know—it just touches me off. I swear to God sometimes it gets so intense I can understand how someone might shake their kid until its head popped off. Not really, but... What's your marriage like? Is it—

KATE: Stop there. No way.

GWEN: Why?

KATE: Why?

GWEN: Are you afraid to talk about your marriage?

KATE: I don't want to. Gwen, marriage is not for talk. Marriage needs no explanation, no qualification, doesn't need to be good or bad. Marriage is marriage is marriage and I'm not going to talk about mine. *(Pause.)* I'd like to give you something.

(She hands GWEN a cheque. GWEN looks at it.)

GWEN: Oh my God. Oh no, no Kate, it's really nice of you but it's too much.

KATE: It's from a bonus. We weren't even expecting it.

GWEN: No, no. Ah, no, Kate—use it to buy a cottage, we'll visit.

(She hands it back. KATE doesn't take it.)

I'm sorry, you're very generous, but...fuck...take it.

(KATE takes the cheque and tears it up.)

You know, a smaller one would do, or...

(KATE hands her a GAP bag.)

KATE: Gracia has the same outfit, in black. I figured Lilly was more of a buttercup kinda girl.

GWEN: Oh it's great, it's so cute. Thank you. She'll look so ah....I'm sorry, I just—

(KATE takes a lighter to the pieces of the cheque. They disappear in a blaze.)

KATE: It never happened.

(Big shift. Sound.

KATE slowly returns upstage to the hotel chair. JOHN F. slowly crosses with tape recorder. We hear snippet of previous scene on speakers.

JOHN exits, KATE sits.)

(Lights shift. JOHN F. offstage.)

KATE: You might be sleeping. At the clinic they told me that eighty percent of insomniacs sleep without knowing it.

(JOHN F. enters with two liqueur glasses, gives one to KATE.)

JOHN F: I—I don't think I'm sleeping.

KATE: I am.

JOHN F: What did they tell you at the clinic?

KATE: Well, it's not technically narcolepsy. And they don't really know anything about narcolepsy anyway. They don't know what causes it.

JOHN F: They don't even know why we sleep.

KATE: I have a fairly good idea what it is in my case.

JOHN F: You do?

KATE: Mmm. It's a way of—a reaction to specific problems and tensions.

JOHN F: Tensions? What kind of uh tensions? If you don't mind me asking.

           (KATE stares off.)

           ...Kate?

KATE: Sorry, I was—

JOHN F: Thinking. You had that thinkin' look you get. What do you think about?

KATE: That will have to remain a mystery to you, I'm afraid.

           (She touches his shirt collar. Pause. Her hand moves languorously down his chest and across his arm as she speaks.)

           So, I'm on some new medication and a regimen of naps that—

JOHN F: A nap— *(He breaks away.)* Sorry, didn't mean to interrupt.

KATE: No, no. It's— And you?

JOHN F: I've tried sleep hygiene, melatonin, acupuncture, herbal teas, various benzodiazapines, everything.

KATE: Hypnosis?

JOHN F: Hypnosis? Ah, no, I don't think I'm... suggestible...that way.

KATE: No maybe not.

JOHN F: I know what my insomnia is. It's connected to this thing I'm working on.

KATE: What thing?

JOHN F: This thing. This novel, this article, this haiku—I don't even know what it is. I spend my nights kind of chewing on it.

KATE: What's it about?

JOHN F: It's not ah, it's not really ah—

KATE: Tell me about it. *(KATE touches him.)*

JOHN F: Well ... *(He moves.)* I'm troubled by, ah, violence.

KATE: How so?

JOHN F: Well I don't understand why more doesn't happen. Why more people don't act out. I mean, there are so many people defeated by power, and revenge is really quite easy. A few phony bomb threats, stink bombs in the stock exchange. It really is easy to vandalize, create mayhem, murder. I mean why did Gordon just kill himself, why didn't he at least take a Tory down with him? *(A pause.)* Sorry.

KATE: That's OK. Go on. You were talking about murder.

JOHN F: *(Moving closer to KATE.)* Well, murder is easy to rationalize. Kill a major shareholder of Nike, they're virtually slave owners. Kidnap and torture a Disney writer—

KATE: Not an executive.

JOHN F: No, William's safe. The point is, all we get are the bombings of abortion clinics. Why? That's what I find curious. The Japanese subway poisoning—why doesn't that happen more often? Why isn't every BMW in North America damaged? Why so many unbroken windows in Rosedale? Why as much order as we have?

KATE: Well, ah, maybe...maybe it's trite, but maybe because it's more convenient to hurt people close by. *(She looks at him. Pause.)*

(Lights and sound shift.)

(GWEN in the big chair. WILLIAM enters demonstrating various martial arts styles.)

WILLIAM: That's Hsing Yi. Then, Bagua has these very round movements, all circles, and Tai Chi is somewhere in the middle: a little angular, a little round.

GWEN: And you have time to practice?

WILLIAM: Well, yeah, a little, half hour, an hour a day.

GWEN: Lucky. I get to do shit. I have no fucking time for anything—sorry, but my life is shit. Oh well.

WILLIAM: You work too hard. The universe wants to play.

GWEN: So do I, I just don't seem to have the time or money or energy.

WILLIAM: Well, we've talked about this. You've got to find a little time, a little light, some joy. Those who hesitate lose their chance at divinity. I, for example, just did a Tantric sex workshop.

GWEN: You did?

WILLIAM: It was very interesting.

GWEN: Now, I read about a Tantric sex workshop in California somewhere.

WILLIAM: The Enlightened Orgasm.

GWEN: That's right. So what was it like? What did you do? If you don't mind me asking.

WILLIAM: Well, we uh, you know, awakened our kundalinis and uh massaged our shakties and—

GWEN: Uh huh. You didn't really do *(Overlaps.)* a workshop—

WILLIAM: *(Overlaps above.)* Ah well—you know, anything to keep you interested... No. Actually, I read the article here at your place, *Elle* magazine.

GWEN: Mirabella. It was Mirabella.

WILLIAM: Of course. A sign of *(Overlaps.)* intelligent life.

GWEN: *(Overlaps above.)* intelligent life—Aha. So you're the one who folded all the pages into little origami—

WILLIAM: Keeps my hands busy, now that I've quit smoking. I also noticed, while I was poking about in your shelves and secret places, I noticed quite a nice little collection of Eastern erotica. What are they called, pillow books?

GWEN: Those are mine.

WILLIAM: I also came across one of John's journals but it was very boring.

GWEN: Tell me about it.

WILLIAM: Do you distinguish between pornography and erotica?

GWEN: You mean... Well, I think it's pretty hard to make absolute rules where images are concerned. But I think that where there's respect between the participants and also the point of view of the image—if it's completely set up for a male viewer, like say in so much industrial or commercial porn... It's uh very odd to be talking to you about this.

WILLIAM: Is it? Why?

GWEN: I'm not sure. I—I don't really know you. I don't know. I never talk to John like this.

WILLIAM: Too bad for John.

GWEN: What about you? Tell me something new. What else are you into these days?

WILLIAM: Me? I'm into hypnosis. *(He dangles a child's toy—a blue ball.)*

GWEN: Hypnosis?

WILLIAM: Hypnosis. Self-hypnosis has helped me quit smoking, improved my golf game by ten strokes and my income by one zero.

GWEN: Really?

WILLIAM: Really.

GWEN: Can you hypnotize other people?

WILLIAM: Sure. There are innumerable induction techniques but there's only one way out. *(Snaps his fingers.)*

GWEN: Really? That's how they do it?

WILLIAM: That's how I do it. But it's not—the thing about hypnosis, the fascinating thing about hypnosis, is that it requires complicity on the part of the hypnotic subject. There are, therefore, limits to what people will do under hypnosis. So called moral limits. It's very interesting.

GWEN: So...could you hypnotize me?

WILLIAM: Don't know. Do you want to be hypnotized?

(He dangles the blue ball. She smiles. He hypnotizes her.)

Light shift.)

(JOHN F. kneels beside KATE, who sits in the small chair. Slowly she touches his hair, his forehead, his lips, pulls him toward her. Lips approach lips. She stops him, takes his hand, and leads him downstage. She turns and exits. He stops. Considers. Takes a big breath and follows her. WILLIAM appears suddenly in front of him. JOHN F. stops. WILLIAM takes JOHN F.'s liqueur glass from him and drains it of its contents. WILLIAM snorts

derisively, then exits. The sound of catcalls and hisses begins to fill the room. JOHN F. alone. Humiliation. He exits. Shift.)

(KATE sits in the big chair reading Mirabella. *JOHN F. enters upstage.)*

JOHN F: *(Behind her.)* Oh hi.

KATE: Do you think I'm impressed?

JOHN F: Sorry?

KATE: I'm not. *(Without turning to him.)*

I'm not impressed by what you do or say, never have been. I suppose that is evident. I've done what you wanted me to do. I'll even go on the trip, it doesn't bother me. I am impervious. I wonder why I can't love you. We have a good life, I feel we've built a fine life together. So why can't I love you anymore? I've lost my capacity to love. I say I love you to Gracia but it's automatic. I can't love anymore. Maybe when we…

(She turns and sees JOHN F.)

KATE: Oh, sorry. *(Turns away.)* I thought you were someone else.

JOHN F: I am someone else.

KATE: John. You're John.

JOHN F: I am a different John with you than I am with Gwen.

KATE: Spare me John, please.

JOHN F: Just as you are a different Kate in my mind than you are in that chair.

KATE: And who am I in that confused head of yours?

JOHN F: A woman of grace and beauty, unable to put a foot wrong, a mountain of resolve and moral symmetry, able to leap tall buildings in a single bound, sharp as a tack. I could have gone on in the past but as I've gotten to know you better you have become someone else, you've become human, tired even, and I see the shadow of regret passing over your luminous face and— If there is anything I can do to help you, ever, just ask. You know, I've never told you before, but I look up to you, to you and William, I envy the clarity of your love. I place you in the pantheon of matrimony, Gods in the Republic of Love, and, somehow, love you both very much and would do—would give my life for you Kate, I— Kate, I can't imagine you have any feelings—

(He is beside her now. He notices she has fallen asleep. He regards her. Then shakes the chair. She wakes.)

KATE: I'm sorry, what were you—

JOHN F: That's all right, nothing... Where's Gwen?

KATE: Oh, Gwen and William are upstairs fucking.

(JOHN F. laughs. Then hears the sounds of lovemaking. Dashes off. Enters further upstage. He looks offstage. The sounds of love grow in volume and intensity. Shadows move rhythmically on his face. Climax. Shadows slow. WILLIAM enters, doing up belt. He looks at JOHN F. and exits. GWEN enters wrapped in a bed sheet. She looks at JOHN F.)

GWEN: Nothing has changed. You'll never love me unless I'm perfect. You're right. I'm a poor excuse for a woman. I'm an infant. Fear rules my life. Anger rules my life. Resentment blinds me. I'm really not cut out for anything. I came into this relationship with nothing but debt and now my tits are sagging and I'm too shy to fuck. You're right, you're absolutely right, you've been right all along.

I'm tired of you, I'm tired of walking on eggshells, I'm tired of your punishments, I'm tired of your lectures, I'm tired of never being made love to... Say something... I'm going to Japan with William and Kate. I'm taking Lilly.

JOHN F: Just like that.

GWEN: Yes. The tickets are bought. We're leaving with Lilly. Tonight.

(He moves to touch her. She evades and exits. From offstage the sheet is thrown in his face. WILLIAM crosses downstage. JOHN F. watches. KATE stands and crosses slowly further downstage. The big chair is removed. WILLIAM exits. KATE exits. WILLIAM enters, takes bed sheet from JOHN F., hands JOHN F. a clipboard and pencil. Exits. JOHN F. signs paper. KATE enters, takes clipboard, exits. WILLIAM enters, places a microphone centre stage. The sound builds. On tape: "WAKE UP." WILLIAM throws JOHN F. to the mic and exits. Sound of impatient crowd. JOHN F., alone, begins immediately speaking to audience.)

JOHN: Good evening ladies and gentlemen. The reason I have brought us all together— I should introduce myself first. My name is John... F. The reason I've brought us all together is that I would like— tonight—tonight we would like to summon—get this—the Devil.

A devil. A demon. To demolish the world; to change the world as we know it. Because the world as we know it needs changing. Oh yes. You know it. I know it. We know it. Some people wouldn't agree. They don't want change.

There are Secret Societies. There are. Conspiracies.

There are—rooms in New York where they secretly scheme to make more money; rooms in Berlin where they secretly study how to make cigarettes more addictive; rooms in Montreal where they secretly conduct experiments on the brains of the unsuspecting; rooms in Jakarta, Moscow, Washington where they secretly plot murder. And rooms in Toronto where couples secretly chew on each other's hearts. Secrets. In rooms.

But let's not have any secrets between us. Let us form our own secret society. And let us agree that the world needs changing.

OK? So, a few things before we uh—just a couple of guidelines, rules to live by, ah, protocols, 27 protocols to live by, to help us along in our quest.

Protocol one: No smoking.

Because tobacco is one of the greatest evils the corporate world has ever unleashed. No smoking.

Protocol Two: No wife jokes.

No Newfie, knock-knock, light bulb, shrink jokes. No kike jokes, no fag or dyke jokes. No wife jokes. Gwendolyn is my wife. I hate my wife. No, ha, I love my wife. Take my wife, please. No wife jokes.

Because I would like to show you something, something scary, something true.

By the by...is there anybody in this room who wants one thing very badly, has wanted one thing very badly—achingly—for many years and know that you simply will never have it, cannot possibly ever have the one thing you want?

Protocol Three: Do not allow the Holocaust into your homes, into your hearts. Because it happens.

By the by...anybody in the room on drugs? Marijuana, caffeine, margarine, nicotine, valium, coca cola, love, anger, prozac? Just curious. Gwen tried prozac for two weeks but she got depressed because it wasn't working.

It doesn't work. The world doesn't work. None of it works. Capitalism—it doesn't work. Communism doesn't work; consumerism doesn't work, poverty doesn't work. Work doesn't work—well, it hasn't worked for me, I don't know about you. Democracy doesn't work; the laws of this nation do not work. Tonight, in this room, let us agree that the laws of this irredeemably corrupt land—and please let's not quibble—the laws of this land no longer apply to us, shall we? OK? Excellent! So...

Protocol Four: The suspension of the Criminal Code.

Oh, wouldn't it be nice. No rules, no laws, anything goes. KLEZMER!

(Klezmer music plays. JOHN F. strikes a pose. Quick cut.)

I used to be innocent, but then I started to want ... things. So I went looking for a devil to sell my soul to, but I couldn't find one who was interested in doing business with me, my soul is far too ... Years later it came to me. I'd already sold it, only I hadn't realized because I sold it so cheap.

Anybody else in the room make the mistake of selling their life for a bargain price? A few shekels, a career advancement, a nice house, a firm thigh, a flake of fame, an answer to a question, worst of all to avoid embarrassment? Anybody else sell their life to avoid embarrassment? ...Anybody make any mistakes? No? I'm probably the only one in the room. Anybody on a drug to make you thin, a drug to make you forget the one thing you most want but can never have? Any body else sell their life because they were too lazy to say no? ...Yes.

Because we are lazy. Lazy, self-involved, greedy fuckin' peevish whining fucks. That's us. Worried about our careers and our natural fibres and our cafe au lait and our websites and parking spots and neo-pagan piercings and our goddamn fertility, and happiness— Who cares? Who promised us any peace, any grace, anything good? What made us think we deserved a goddamn thing. Hence ...

Protocol five: The end of rights.

The right to own a car, the right to own a TV, the right to go to the movies, the right to buy as much cheap plastic shit as you want, the right to cabs and a steady stream of buses and conveniences and sauces and CDs and your drug of choice and your delight in graceful words, your right to be kept alive well past your usefulness.

As of tonight, we in this room, together, this evening, we deny the right to Right, we abrogate eradicate defabricate this fabrication of Rights. Tonight, in this dirty dirty room, there are no rights, you have no right to anything. Demon, take it away. Please.

Protocol six: no more cars.

Protocol seven: no more advertising.

Protocol eight: no more marriage.

Protocol nine: no more babies in this filthy world.

Protocol ten...Doubt.

(Sound.)

Doubt.

How can you know? How can you be sure? "A person never knows."

You don't know, for example, the poisons you

ingest day to day. The chemicals that accelerate death to weeds, death to insects, also accelerate growth to chickens, accelerate the udders of cows to bovine bursting, accelerating beyond thought to death.

(Sound of glass breaking.)

You don't know what cancer you are breathing in this dirty room, ticking minutes off your life with each second accelerating death. The acceleration of books and knowledge and more and more and multicultural high speed high yield low overhead global move and motion all acceleration. Go for it Disney, go for it Nike, go for it Time Warner. "Time Warner." But who hears the warning? Too much cancer in the inner vestibula.

And you don't know how you became what you are in the Republic of Doubt. You don't know who makes most of your decisions for you in this Republic of Doubt. You don't know who is playing with your child's brain or who played with yours when you were a tyke. CIA brain washing, the Catholic church, the PR budget of your government—we spend more on advertising than education, we build cities for cars. The collusion of bankers and the US Congress and the Zionist state and idiot Arafat and the arrogance of this ignorant Conservative juggernaut and the bottom line of even the leftist of the liberal and laborers voting for the men in suits and Christians schooling their kids at home and I tell you, the radical right paramilitary and the radical anarcho left sleep in the same forests. Ernst Zundel, Ralph Nadar, Louis Farrakhan, they all preach to the same hole in the tumorous soul of Democracy.

(Sound is building.)

Demon, enter the soul of this room and destroy any goodness we may have left. Make us hate the person we sit beside, hate our lives, our work, our country, our language, hate our beliefs. Demon, enter now and destroy the last vestiges of Democracy, make us see the futility, the duplicitous dissembling, the weakness, fire us with your strength, your loathsome power, your fear destroying grandeur, your phallic enormity, your stench and sensual overwhelm. And no one knows, no one knows in the Republic of Doubt, and why, I've been good, why can't I get a good nights sleep, I've been so good, all I want is a good nights sleep, Demon, give me sleep, give me rest, sleep, rest, please, that's all, really, that's all...

(Silence.)

...Sorry... Sorry Gwen... Sorry.

(He continues with composure.)

Protocol eleven: an end to wage slavery.

Protocol twelve: *(He loses composure.)* the dirty room.

Protocol thirteen: see protocol fourteen.

Protocol fourteen: ignore protocol thirteen.

Protocol fifteen: ignore all future protocols.

Protocol sixteen: ignore all past protocols.

Protocol seventeen: protocol seventeen: protocol seventeen: protocol seventeen: protocol seventeen: protocol seventeen: protocol seventeen...

(With Protocol seventeen GWEN begins speaking Japanese offstage. Slowly crosses the stage wearing a kimono.)

GWEN: Anatawa totemo yasashi desu.
Mada Yoko machigaimasu

Tokidoki anata no kotoba o dame ni
Shiteiru to yu Kiga suru.

(The microphone is removed as JOHN F. continues Protocol seventeen and begins to twitch and move.)

Omosheiroi Desho?
(Laughs.) Zenbu, watashino Hanashi
Kata toka
Kono kimono toka. Tada, totemo utsukuhii desu
Ko Yu Shizuka sa, tanjunsa, ureshii desu

(She exits as she speaks. The sound of ticking, a train, JOHN F. alone.)

(JOHN F. is alone. Music, sound, JOHN F. searches, standing on the spot, twitching, looking for an answer, looking for sleep. He rocks and fidgets and caresses himself. He breathes deeply and tries to calm himself. He prays. He punches the air, the sound of breaking glass as he looks for sleep, fidgets, walks a tight square, jumps quarter-turns and punches glass, rocks, takes pencils from his jacket and writes on floor, rocks and punches, breaking glass, jumps and turns, breathes, writes with pencils more pencils, desperately punches glass, erases, paces, writes, erases, punches glass, tries to sleep, exhausted, takes cassette from pocket and pulls out the tape, unwinds metres and metres of tape, sound of rewind, syncopated ticking, he makes a pillow with tape, lies down and tries to sleep, removes his jacket, carefully shapes it into a pillow over tape, gently lays his head on it, tries to sleep, music continues, punches, writes, lays on his back, rocks, the sound of a phone ringing far away, fitfully rocks from side to side and rocks, sound, ticking, his fingers twitch, the phone grows louder, he rocks, suddenly all music stops.

The phone rings. JOHN F. sits up.)

KATE:	*(From offstage, through mic effect as if on phone)* Hi John.
JOHN F:	Kate.
KATE:	*(On mic.)* John. It's been a long time. We've all been through some real changes. We're coming into town. Let's have dinner. At your place.
JOHN F:	Kate, I'm not—where are you?
KATE:	*(On mic.)* California. We're just back from Japan.
JOHN F:	Kate, I'm—I've been in jail.
KATE:	*(On mic.)* Oh good, you'll have to tell us all about it. John, it's time to put the pieces back together.
JOHN F:	Kate, I, I'd love to see you. Is—is Gwen coming?
KATE:	*(On mic.)* Yes, yes of course. She wants to see you.

(Sound of alarm. JOHN F. slowly rises to standing. Alarm stops.)

JOHN F: Protocol twenty seven: the possibility of redemption.

(JOHN F. exits slowly, muttering.

A dinner table appears.)

(The table is set and dinner is ready. KATE, GWEN, and WILLIAM are all at table. Waiting. JOHN F. arrives late.)

JOHN F: *(Standing.)* Sorry I'm late, inexcusable, punishable under Section 46 of the Criminal Code. Sorry Gwen, forgive me. *(Noticing food.)* You've cooked...

(GWEN looks at him and doesn't speak.)

KATE: John, did you get a haircut?

JOHN F:	No, I just bathed.
KATE:	Well, it looks very nice.
WILLIAM:	Why don't you sit down?
JOHN F:	Uh sure. Good idea. *(Sits.)* How is everyone?
GWEN & KATE:	Good. Fine.
WILLIAM:	Hungry.
JOHN F:	Well good, everyone is in fine fettle. Um, meal looks great, thanks Gwen.
GWEN:	I hope it tastes as good as it looks.
WILLIAM:	I'm sure it will.
JOHN F:	OK. OK. *(He grabs his glass and stands.)*
	Well … I've been, uh—I'm just so ah… It's … I'm—
	(KATE takes his hand. He stops.)
	To you—to us.
	(They all toast.)
GWEN:	Dive in. It tastes like cement if you don't eat it hot.
	(They dive in. Appreciative noises.)
JOHN F:	So, how is Gracia?
KATE:	She's fine, although our cat killed our hamster.
JOHN F:	Oh my God that's terrible.
KATE:	See, that's the kind of response I want.
WILLIAM:	But you hate the hamster.
KATE:	It is still a part of our family, as low down on the food chain as it might be. Have some compassion.
WILLIAM:	For a hamster?

KATE: Your capacity for compassion should be infinite.

WILLIAM: My love for you is infinite, the Gods are jealous and that is why there is suffering in the world.

KATE: That may be so William but love will not breathe life into that hamster.

WILLIAM: It breathes life into me.

KATE: I can't be held responsible for that.

(They notice JOHN F. and GWEN looking at one another.)

...This is good, what is it?

GWEN: A Jewish stew, all organic ingredients.

KATE: What is that...that...?

GWEN: That's the flavour of the meat.

KATE: What kind of meat is it?

GWEN: I don't know... *(Very puzzled.)* I don't know.

WILLIAM: C'mon Gwen, snap out of it.

(He snaps his fingers, she snaps out of it.)

GWEN: What?

JOHN F: What kind of meat?

(She is very distracted.)

It's good. You don't believe— She thinks its bullshit when I say that because I never used to say it and now—

(GWEN stands and leaves the table.)

What's wrong? What's—

(GWEN exits. Offstage she rummages frantically,

looking for something. JOHN F. excuses himself and moves offstage.)

JOHN F: *(Offstage.)* What's wrong?

GWEN: *(Off.)* I just want to get dinner on the table.

JOHN F: *(Off.)* It is on the table.

KATE: *(Overlaps JOHN F. and GWEN.)* What's up?

WILLIAM: She lost the recipe, I don't know. It's good though. Eat, you're looking pale.

GWEN: *(Off.)* That's all right.

JOHN F: *(Off.)* Did I say something wrong or—?

GWEN: *(Off.)* No no, you just go back to the table, I'm fine.

(JOHN F. returns to the table, sits.)

WILLIAM: What's going on?

JOHN F: I don't know.

(GWEN offstage, on phone.)

GWEN: *(Off.)* Hi Cheryl, hi, is is Lilly there? She's—I don't know where she is. I don't know where I left her, I don't know where I left her .... No, no, I think—I don't remember where she is—I don't know where I put her—

JOHN F: *(To KATE and WILLIAM, overlaps.)* Do you know where Lilly is?

GWEN: *(Off, overlaps.)* I left her—I don't know where she is—

(Hangs up.)

KATE: *(Overlaps.)* I don't know.

WILLIAM: Don't know— I thought she was having dinner with the twins. What's their names?

(GWEN crosses upstage.)

JOHN F: Gwen, where's Lilly?

GWEN: *(As she crosses.)* I DON'T KNOW.

(JOHN F. quickly exits. We hear smashing of pots and pans. WILLIAM continues to eat. JOHN F. dials offstage.)

JOHN F: *(Offstage.)* Hi Alan? Is Lilly at your place? No? No, never mind. Yeah—no, I'm in a bit of a hurry, I'll call you later…yeah…yeah, no, but I've got to run …sure sure, but I should call you back later— Oh yeah, everything's fine, yeah…yeah. OK…OK bye.

(Hangs up, dashes across stage.)

Gwen, what is it?

GWEN: *(Screams.)* LEAVE ME ALONE.

(GWEN crosses slowly, over and over. JOHN F. crosses frantically, over and over. Music mounts.)

JOHN F: What? What is it?

(GWEN crosses, JOHN F. crosses. Like a furious ballet. The crosses accelerate. WILLIAM continues to eat. KATE suddenly stands and backs away from the table, staring at her plate. JOHN F. running madly crosses upstage of her.)

What?…

(WILLIAM stifles a laugh. JOHN F. runs, shouting "what?", and "GWEN, what is it?" GWEN approaches the table, terrified, slowly, slowly. She arrives at the table, stares into the pot of food, and keens. JOHN F. arrives at the table, music loud, GWEN keening, JOHN F. pounding the table "what, what, what…"

Sudden silence. Three screams from GWEN, then…

Lights shift. The sound of wind. A bell. A train. Voices. Darkness. Terror. Time. Quiet. Ticking.)

(The table disappears. JOHN F. sitting on floor. GWEN circles him, then sits. They are alone. Ticking.)

GWEN: You've been funny today.

JOHN F: How so?

GWEN: You've been nice to me.

JOHN F: Well, I had a...I've been wondering lately about love...and I've been wondering about how long it lasts.

GWEN: And?

JOHN F: I'm wondering if there's anything longer than forever.

GWEN: Forever's pretty good.

(They touch. Pause.)

Is there anything longer than forever?

JOHN F: Well, scientists are working on that one, angels are praying for it, and sinners are dreading it.

GWEN: Sinners?

JOHN F: Sinners, like you and me.

GWEN: I thought we were lovers.

JOHN F: Tonight we are. But you never know what's gonna wake up beside you in the morning.

GWEN: Then let's not wake up. Let's sleep forever.

(They kiss.)

A knock on the door. The kiss concludes.. GWEN goes to answer the door. Kate and William have arrived. JOHN F. comes to greet them. Hellos and hugs and kisses and chat about the flight and a present of rare liquor. Dialogue semi-improvised. A different feel than what has come before.)

KATE: *(To WILLIAM.)* Honey, we're going up and see the baby.

WILLIAM: OK, I'll be there in a minute.

(KATE and GWEN exit to see Lilly.)

So, how are you doing John?

JOHN: Oh, you know…I started smoking again… I'll buy you some drinks and we can talk.

WILLIAM: OK. I'm going up see the baby.

(Grunts as he lifts the suitcases, exits to baby room.

JOHN F. is alone, his back to the audience. In the distance we hear GWEN and KATE cooing over the baby. JOHN F. turns downstage. He is holding a baby monitor. We hear GWEN, KATE and WILLIAM through the monitor. JOHN F. slowly approaches the audience, listening to the monitor. The dialogue is semi-improvised.)

(Full voice.) Let me see the little Johnny …

(KATE shushes him.)

Oh. Sorry.

GWEN: Oh, she sleeps through anything.

WILLIAM: Oh, Gwen, she has your nose.

GWEN: You think so? That makes you a lucky little girl.

KATE: Honey, look, they put up the mobile we sent from Japan.

GWEN: We love it …

KATE: William picked that out.

GWEN: Oh, look, her eyelids are fluttering. I think Lilly's having a little dream.

WILLIAM: She's dreaming?

(JOHN F. is downstage, calmly facing the audience. GWEN begins to sing a lullaby. KATE and WILLIAM talk sparingly, quietly, in background.)

GWEN: *(Singing.)* Who's gonna shoe your pretty little feet?
Who's gonna glove your little hand.
And who's gonna kiss, your ruby red lips?
Oooo, ooo, ooo, ooo.

(JOHN F. listens face to face with audience. Takes a big breath and closes his eyes. The lights begin to fade as GWEN sings.)

Poppa's gonna shoe your pretty little feet.
Momma's gonna glove your little hands.
And I'm gonna kiss your ruby red lips.
Ooo, ooo, ooo, ooo.

(Lights fade to black. Only the red light of the baby monitor glows. Pause.

The red light clicks off. Quiet.)

The End

GWEN:	We love it …
KATE:	William picked that out.
GWEN:	Oh, look, her eyelids are fluttering. I think Lilly's having a little dream.
WILLIAM:	She's dreaming?

(JOHN F. is downstage, calmly facing the audience. GWEN begins to sing a lullaby. KATE and WILLIAM talk sparingly, quietly, in background.)

GWEN: (*Singing.*) Who's gonna shoe your pretty little feet?
Who's gonna glove your little hand.
And who's gonna kiss, your ruby red lips?
Oooo, ooo, ooo, ooo.

(JOHN F. listens face to face with audience. Takes a big breath and closes his eyes. The lights begin to fade as GWEN sings.)

Poppa's gonna shoe your pretty little feet.
Momma's gonna glove your little hands.
And I'm gonna kiss your ruby red lips.
Ooo, ooo, ooo, ooo.

(Lights fade to black. Only the red light of the baby monitor glows. Pause.

The red light clicks off. Quiet.)

The End